Steaming M

Want that Perfect Latte or Cappuccino?

By

Jessica Simms

Steaming Milk: Want that Perfect Latte or Cappuccino?

Copyright © 2017

ISBN: 9781549669323

Warning and Disclaimer

Publisher Contact

Skinny Bottle Publishing

books@skinnybottle.com

The Importance of Milk

If you start out your day with a black coffee or shot of espresso, studying up on blends, roast levels, and brewing practices will give you the knowledge you need to make your perfect cup at home. If your drink of choice is a latte or a cappuccino, however, the preparation of the coffee is only half the story. The steamed milk that makes up the bulk of these drinks is just as important to the flavor and texture.

Making your own lattes and cappuccinos at home can be a more daunting task than brewing up your own quality coffee. Most people don't have access to an espresso machine, and even those who do own them rarely have a commercial, dual-boiler model at their disposal, making it more difficult to get the finely-textured milk you'd find in a café. If you've ever tried heating your own milk for coffee drinks on the stove or in a microwave, you know that there is more to the process of steaming than just quickly and evenly heating the milk. The rapid incorporation of air creates froth and sweetens the milk, making milk that has been heated but not steamed taste flat in comparison.

Because of the movement of steam through it, the milk produced on a steaming pitcher will be a mix of heated, liquid milk and stiffer foam, with bubbles of air trapped in the milk's fats and proteins. Correctly steamed milk will complement the flavor of a great espresso shot, bringing out its more nuanced flavors and enhancing the texture; poorly steamed milk can give the drink either a grainy or a foamy texture or make the drink feel heavy and dull.

While the foam and steamed milk will be thoroughly incorporated if the steaming is done correctly, they will eventually separate out into separate components if left to sit and can be thought of as separate byproducts of the steaming process for practical purposes. The difference between most of the drinks you'll find on café menus has to do with the ratio of foam to steamed milk to coffee, and the accompanying changes in technique creating those different textures will necessitate.

There are techniques and tools you can use to steam your own milk at home, even if your coffee budget doesn't have room for a commercial espresso machine. Even if you don't plan on preparing your own milk at home, though, learning a bit about the science and technique behind the different drinks on the café menu will help you to order exactly what you're looking for. This is especially important if you're trying to avoid dairy, as the various alternative milk types on the market can give you very different results when they're steamed and combined with espresso. If you do decide to experiment with steaming your own milk at home, you may be surprised by how simple it is to learn the basic techniques—and how difficult it can be to master the art of the perfect steam.

Milk Steaming Basics

There is more to the operation of the steam wand on an espresso machine than simply heating the milk to the right temperature. As you might have inferred from the name, it uses high-pressure steam to heat the milk, similar to how the espresso is forced out of the group head. In addition to quickly heating the milk, this steam incorporates air bubbles into the milk, creating the silky smooth foam that is so integral to a high-quality latte or cappuccino.

The basic premise behind quality microfoam is the same as the science behind the crema that goes on top of an espresso shot. The smooth, glossy foam is the result of tiny air bubbles that are suspended in the liquid by the high pressure of the steam wand. With crema, this happens because carbon dioxide and other gasses are released from the ground beans by the heat of the steam and are unable to escape the portafilter and they become trapped in the brewing coffee, where they're suspended in the liquid. With steamed milk, the bubbles are formed by allowing air to be introduced into the milk during the steaming process, which is

3

then encased in the sugars and proteins and trapped inside the liquid.

Milk that has been correctly steamed should have the appearance of wet paint, or "white chrome" as you may hear in the barista community, with a reflective sheen and no visible bubbles. The smooth, silky texture this surface indicates will blend quite nicely with the espresso in drinks like lattes and cappuccinos. The key to achieving this texture is to get just the right amount of air incorporated into the milk. If the tip of the wand is inserted too deep into the milk, not enough air will be worked in, resulting in milk that's heated but with no increase in volume and no foam on top. Putting the tip too close to the surface will allow too much air in, resulting in large bubbles that don't mix into the milk. The goal is to find a middle ground and pull a steady, small stream of air into the milk. Gradually introducing the steam into the milk will cause the fats, proteins, and sugars in the milk to expand as they create the finely-textured microfoam.

Steaming supplies

There are a variety of ways that you can make frothed milk. An espresso machine's steam wand is the most reliable means, but there are other options. Some of these will heat the milk as it froths it, while others will require a secondary heating source; there is more information on all the different means of steaming, frothing, and heating milk later in this book.

Regardless of which method you use to steam the milk, however, there are a few other supplies that you'll find helpful in crafting perfectly steamed and textured milk. This list is far less extensive than the various supplies you'll need for making a quality cup of coffee—in fact, there are only two main supplies you'll want to get specifically for milk: a thermometer and a steaming pitcher.

The thermometers used by baristas in cafes when they steam their milk are specialized in the sense that they are designed for use with milk, but are relatively low-tech and inexpensive, typically costing less than five bucks each. They use a standard analog temperature dial, usually with the ideal steaming zone marked in a distinctive color on the face. Even if you own a digital thermometer already, buying a thermometer specifically for your milk steaming is a good idea. The digital read-out may not update quickly enough to catch your milk at exactly the right temperature. Milk thermometers can also be easily reset to ensure their accuracy using the hexagonal tool that comes included in the package. Testing its temperature reading is equally easy; simply place the probe end in a glass of ice, then adjust until the thermometer reads 32°F.

Milk thermometers are designed to clip onto the side of your pitcher, with the probe end angled in such a way that it doesn't touch either the wand itself or the side of the pitcher while it's steaming. You may see baristas steaming milk without the use of a thermometer, judging the temperature of the milk simply by the heat of the pitcher against their palm. As you gain practice this can be an effective way of judging the correct steaming temperature, but even experienced baristas will use a thermometer to periodically check the temperature of their drink, and this is certainly a good idea when you're first learning the process.

You will also need a pitcher to steam your milk in unless you're using a jug-style frother. Steaming pitchers are made of thin-walled metal for maximum durability and heat transfer, with a spout on one side for pouring the milk and a handle on the other, for more convenient holding. They come in a variety of sizes, but three are most common: 8-ounce pitchers (typically used for small drinks, like cortados and macchiatos), 12-ounce pitchers (used for lattes and cappuccinos), and 20-ounce pitchers (generally employed for large, dry cappuccinos or steaming multiple drinks at once).

A good rule of thumb is to use the smallest pitcher that you can to effectively steam your milk without it overflowing as the volume increases. If you're not sure what size of pitcher you need, the best choice is to default to a 12-ounce model. You can steam milk for a latte or cappuccino in an 8-ounce pitcher, but it won't give you much room for error and you're likely to make quite a mess when you're first starting out. A 20-ounce pitcher, on the other hand, will be too large to get a good steam on your milk unless you're making a large quantity. Using the correct pitcher size helps to control the surface area and depth of the milk, ensuring an even steam.

The steaming process

Regardless of what type of device you're using to steam your milk, there are a few pieces of advice that will help you to achieve consistently good results. First, it's important to always start with cold milk in a cold pitcher. Ideally, both should be around 34°F, or just above freezing. Once the milk gets above around 100°F, the proteins will break down, which releases the air you're trying to incorporate and makes it impossible to get the smooth, creamy microfoam you want for espresso drinks. Be mindful of the weather outside when you're making your drinks, too. Humidity has more of an impact on the quality of your espresso shots than it will on your milk, but especially cold or hot weather will alter the amount of time it requires to steam.

There is also a consistently ideal temperature for milk across methods. You should steam your milk to somewhere between 140°F and 170°F. While different cafes and recipes will list different exact temperatures as their standard or ideal, anything within that range will be both delicious and have sufficient microfoam for making latte art. Anything that's too cold will taste chalky and won't have the sweetness of steamed milk; anything that's too hot will be scalded and will lose much of its best flavor.

Steaming milk causes a series of changes to the chemical composition of the beverage. The longer chain carbohydrates naturally present in milk will break down into simpler sugars as a result of the heat, which makes them easier to taste, enhancing the perceived sweetness of the beverage. The addition of heat will also cause the tightly coiled bundles of protein in the milk to unwind.

7

These proteins are hydrophobic (water-repellent) on one side, and hydrophilic (water attracted) on the other. When these uncoiled proteins encounter the air bubbles you've worked into the milk, the hydrophobic side wraps around the air, while the hydrophilic side binds it to the surrounding liquid. This is ultimately what forms the structure of the microfoam. If the milk gets above a certain temperature, the proteins will break down further and will no longer be able to form the protective layer around the air bubbles. This is the main reason why it's important to start your milk from a cold temperature.

You don't necessarily need to know the science behind milk steaming in order to make a delicious latte or cappuccino, but understanding why the milk reacts to heat and air the way it does can help you to troubleshoot your milk when you have problems. The specific details of timing and temperature will vary depending on the kind of drink you're making, the kind of milk you're using, the tools you have for frothing, and your own personal tastes.

Choosing a Milk

As recently as the 1990s, a customer at a coffee shop looking for a non-dairy option would most likely need to stick to teas or black coffee; even soy milk, though available, was not widely utilized in most shops. In most cases, the only decision you would have to make regarding the milk in your coffee would be whether you wanted to use whole or skim.

The number of milk options available to consumers has greatly expanded in the years since. This is great news to those with dietary restrictions but can make things significantly more complicated from the steaming side of the equation. Each milk option will have its own advantages and drawbacks when it comes to the steamed texture, and each will impart its own distinctive flavor to the drink.

Dairy options

When it comes to cow's milk, the bulk of the liquid—around 87% by volume—is comprised of water. The remainder of the volume is a mix of proteins, sugars, and fats, with the ratio between them varying depending on the kind of milk you're using. The standard labeling of cow's milk makes it fairly easy to determine just what is contained in each variety. Non-fat milk has virtually no fat since it's skimmed off the top before the milk is bottled (hence the alternative name of "skim milk"). If there is a percentage on the label, that refers to the included fat (e.g. 1% or 2%), while "whole milk" usually contains between 4% and 6% fat. Beyond that is half and half, which is made up of half whole milk and half cream, followed by heavy cream or whipping cream, which will have the thickest texture and the highest fat content.

All of the milk you find in the grocery store is likely to be homogenized, which is a production process that distributes the fat more evenly throughout the beverage. In non-homogenized milk, the fat will be floating around in globules of various sizes within the liquid portion of the beverage, often forming into a fat cap at the top of the jug of milk. The homogenization process involves forcing the milk through a small nozzle, which breaks up the fat and distributes it more evenly throughout. Homogenized milk will give you a far superior texture after steaming, and is necessary if you want to use your milk to make latte art.

Dairy products contain a special sugar, called lactose, that's not found in any other food. This is the component of milk that people who are lactose intolerant have an adverse reaction to and is also what makes the milk sweet when it's fresh and sour when it's not. The typical lactose content in milk is around 4-5%, regardless of the level of milk fat.

If the level of milk fat in your beverage isn't an issue for you health-wise, determining the right fat content for the drink you're making will depend both on what kind of drink it is and the taste that you prefer in your beverage. Skim milk will be the easiest to form into a stiff and persistent foam, which makes it excellent for cappuccinos. If you're trying to make latte art, however, the foam has a tendency to get too thick and to clump, which can prevent you from making as detailed or nice of a design. Whole milk, on the other hand, brings a lovely decadent taste to the drink and can create very silky microfoam that's perfect for lattes, even if the foam won't be as firm as with a non-fat milk. While whole milk is the default in most cafes, for many baristas a 1% or 2% milk is the ideal balance between taste, texture, and consistency.

Alternative milk

The difference between skim and whole cow's milk is definitely noticeable, both in terms of the taste and the texture, but this difference is nothing compared to that between the various types of non-dairy milk that are available on the modern market. More options seem to pop up all the time, and each will impart its own distinctive flavor to your beverages—and present its own unique challenges when it comes time to add the steam.

As a general rule, alternative milks don't steam as nicely as cow's milk. This is largely because of the lower fat content. You can find various alternative milks that are specifically formulated for use by baristas. These versions will steam better than other milks of the same variety, and an experienced barista can still achieve excellent results with many of them, but they will still typically require more grooming than cow's milk, will be more difficult to foam and will have a noticeable taste that can clash with some coffees, especially brighter and more complex single-origin espressos.

There are a few alternative kinds of milk that you should steer clear of as a rule when you're making espresso-based drinks. Rice milk has a subtle flavor that blends well with coffee, but it's one of the thinnest of the alternative milks, and will produce virtually no foam; the same is true of oat milk. Coconut milk, on the other hand, is thicker and contains slightly more fat. It can produce respectable foam in the right hands, even creating respectable latte art, but many people find its taste after steaming to be off-putting and to clash with the flavor of coffee.

As with choosing a milk fat level with cow's milk, picking the right alternative milk will be a matter of both the type of drink you're making and your preferences from a taste perspective. Your best options will fall into three categories: soy, hemp, and nut milks. Each of these categories will have its own advantages and drawbacks, which are explored in more detail below.

Soy milk

Soy was the original non-dairy milk offered in cafes and remains the most widely available option. In the early years of its popularity, it was seen as a healthier alternative to cow's milk. Modern research has started to contradict this belief, and amidst concerns over the sugar and estrogen content of the product, soy milk has fallen slightly out of favor among third-wave coffee shops. Still, if you're looking for a dairy-free, nut-free option, soy remains a popular choice.

The high protein content of soy milk makes it excellent for use with cappuccinos, producing a thick microfoam that doesn't dissipate quickly. This also makes it trickier to use in latte art, however; it will behave similarly to skim milk in this context, providing good contrast in colors but often clumping on the surface, preventing you from getting fine details or sharp lines.

The fact that soy milk has been used in cafes for over two decades gives it the added advantage that there are several varieties on the market specifically designed for use with coffee. You can experiment with different brands and varieties until you find the one that works the best for you. Going with unflavored and unsweetened varieties will have the least impact on the flavor, though it will still taste slightly different than drinks made with regular milk. Soy tends to bring out more of the chocolatey, rich notes of the coffee, even when it's unflavored.

Hemp milk

If your diet restricts you from eating nuts or dairy but you're dubious about the health impact of soy, hemp milk is likely to be your best alternative. It steams very similarly to soy milk and has enough protein for use in cappuccinos. The microfoam is persistent but not as thick as with soy milk, which can actually make it a better option if you want to make latte art, giving you more definition and precision in your lines. Hemp milk also has a higher fat content than soy, meaning it will have more of the creamy, thick texture most people are looking for.

In terms of taste, hemp milk has the most unusual flavor of the alternative milks on this list. It comes from the same plant which is used to make hemp rope, and some varieties will have a very pronounced vegetal, almost woody flavor that some people find off-putting. It is also a more recent addition to the alternative milk roster, which means you're less likely to see it as an option in your local café, and depending on your area may need to seek it out at a specialty grocers or purchase it online rather than finding it on the shelves of your local supermarket.

Nut milks

You'll find a lot of different varieties of milks that are based on nuts. Almond milk is the most widely-available by far, followed by cashew milk; you may also find pistachio or macadamia nut milk in specialty stores, though they will rarely be on offer at your local café. As a general rule, nut milk is thinner than cow's milk, soy milk, or hemp milk. This makes it a poor choice for cappuccinos and macchiatos since the foam will not be particularly stiff or thick. Most people prefer the flavor, however, and it can make some very attractive latte art in the right hands.

In terms of the steaming process, you'll find working with almond milk to be similar to working with skim milk, generating a lot of large bubbles that can make it difficult to achieve consistent, glossy microfoam. You'll also have to be more mindful of your temperatures when working with almond milk. It needs to be aerated early, and shouldn't be allowed to go above 140°F or it runs the risk of scorching. Almond milk is also known to curdle at certain temperatures, which won't affect its taste but can look unappetizing in the cup.

Cashew milk will be similar in its taste and texture to almond milk, though it's slightly sweeter, and will lend the drink a more pronounced nutty flavor. In terms of the texture, it's even thinner than almond milk; when steamed, it will produce very large bubbles, making it almost impossible to achieve a silky microfoam. Of the viable options on this list, it is the least viable option for making either latte art or cappuccinos. Most people who favor cashew milk in coffee drinks do so on the basis of taste. You should also use caution when purchasing cashew milk in the store, as it is often mixed with other nut milks when it's packaged and sold.

The other less common nut milks will have similar taste and texture profiles to almond milk. Macadamia nut milk, if you can find it, is one of the best nut milk options when it comes to

15

steaming; pistachio milk, conversely, is one of the worst. New varieties and formulas are being released on a regular basis, however. If you're on the quest for the perfect non-dairy latte, experimenting with new brands and flavors will be well worth the monetary investment.

Drinks and Terminology

There is a lot of specialized technology associated with coffee, and while this is the case for a variety of food and beverage preparation, understanding coffee lingo can present a unique challenge. Not only are many of the most common terms derived from Italian, but many countries—and even regions within the same country—will have different terms for the same drink. Being able to make an effective cappuccino or macchiato first means understanding exactly what goes into creating that drink, and what the preparation standards are for your particular area.

The third wave of specialty coffee that started in the 1990s has had the beneficial effect of standardizing many of the drink definitions and recipes within the United States, largely thanks to organizations like the Specialty Coffee Association of America and the Barista's Guild. Even so, you may find that particular shops have their own unique methods of preparation, even for common drinks like lattes, which can further confuse the coffee novice.

There are two main factors that will determine the difference between beverage types: the ratio of milk to coffee and the amount of foamed versus steamed milk. In some cases, the differences between beverages are quite subtle; in others, beverages with vastly different tastes and textures will be called the same thing. Understanding the basic features of each drink will help you to prepare your milk correctly.

Café au lait

The au lait is the simplest of the milk-based drinks. You can think of it as a French version of the latte, though it uses drip or immersion brewed coffee in lieu of the espresso. It is a great recipe to start with as a beginner because it is the most forgiving of the drinks on this list. While it will taste better if you use frothed milk, foam is not an integral component of the beverage. This makes it one of the few drinks on this list that can be correctly prepared without a milk frother.

The ideal au lait uses a strong coffee as its base—typically a French roast or similarly dark blend. You want to use a 1:1 ratio of coffee to steamed milk during the preparation. The best blend will be achieved by pouring the milk and coffee into the cup simultaneously, but if this isn't possible, your best bet is to pour the coffee into the cup first, then top it off with the steamed milk.

Caffe latte

Literally translating to "milk coffee," a latte is the first espresso drink any budding barista will learn to make. It is arguably the most popular espresso-based beverage, at least in the United States, and can be prepared easily with a whole host of alternative milks. If the drink is made using steamed half-and-half, it is referred to as a "breve."

A traditional latte uses a coffee to milk ratio of between 1:3 and 1:5. This means for a single shot of espresso, you should use between 3 and 5 ounces of milk; for a double shot, between 6 and 10. On top of this milk will be a small amount of microfoam, which can be combined with the crema on top of the espresso shot to make latte art at the barista's discretion. The espresso should go into the cup first, with the milk poured in on top in a slow, steady stream. If you are adding any flavor syrups, they should be mixed into the espresso for the evener distribution; if you're adding flavored powders, they should be steamed into the milk.

Cappuccino

Once you have mastered the steaming of milk for a latte, you will be ready to advance to the cappuccino. The recipe for a traditional cappuccino calls for equal parts espresso, steamed milk, and foamed milk. If the cappuccino is "dry," it uses more foam than milk; if it is "wet," it uses more milk than foam.

There are multiple ways of preparing a cappuccino. A traditional Italian cappuccino is almost always free-poured, with the ratio of milk to foam controlled by the quality of the barista's steaming. The steamed milk can either be poured into the espresso, or the espresso shots can be poured in through the foam at the end.

In American cafes, a different approach is sometimes favored. Rather than keeping the milk and foam combined in the pitcher, they're allowed to separate. The foam is held back using a spoon, allowing the liquid milk to pour into the cup, after which the foam is spooned on top. This method makes it easier to identify the exact ratio of milk to foam, especially for a relative beginner who isn't quite so confident in their steaming ability. While you will find staunch adherents of each approach, neither one is any more technically correct than the other.

Caffe mocha

The Mocha is a variant of the caffe latte and follows the same basic principle. The only difference is the inclusion of chocolate in the beverage, along with the milk and espresso. This can take a variety of forms. Some people prefer to use chocolate syrup mixed with the espresso; some prefer the taste of powdered cocoa steamed into the milk, and some use a chocolate milk or chocolate crème as the main component. However you prepare it, you should use a similar coffee to milk ratio (1:3 to 1:5) and include a small amount of foam on top.

Macchiato

This term can be a bit confusing because it is used to refer to two different drinks. The word "macchiato" means "marked," and indicates one substance that makes up the primary bulk of the drink which is then finished with a small amount of another component. Whether the espresso or the milk makes up the bulk of the drink is what differentiates the two variations.

An espresso macchiato is an espresso marked by a small amount of foamed milk. This can be a single or a double espresso, on top of which a dollop of foamed milk is added. A latte macchiato is a milk marked by a small amount of espresso. It is similar to a caffe latte but differs in a few key ways. First of all, the milk is foamed more than with a latte, meaning you'll spend more time in the stretching phase. Secondly, you want to pour the milk into the cup first and then pour the espresso down through it to finish it off. The surface will be mostly white with a dot of brown in the center. It is also typically served as a layered drink rather than being stirred, so you may want to serve it in a glass cup to show this off.

Any macchiato that uses a syrup flavor is going to be a variant on the latte macchiato. A caramel macchiato, for example, will have a layer of caramel syrup below the milk, with a drizzle of caramel over the top, typically in a grid-like pattern. Again, the difference between this and a flavored latte has to do with the layering of the flavors and the texture of the milk.

Cortado

The word "cortado" means "cut" in Italian, and describes a drink that uses an espresso to milk ratio of about 1:1. You can think of it a little bit like a small latte, though there are a few key differences beyond simply the ratio. The milk for a cortado is typically steamed a little cooler than for lattes—around 140°F is considered ideal. The amount of foam in the milk is often a matter of personal taste. Some like their cortados more steamed, while others prefer a more latte-like layer of microfoam on the top.

Flat white

This is an Australian variant of the cappuccino. Invented in the 1980s, it has only recently gained more international acclaim. The flat white was designed as an alternative to the foamy Italian-style cappuccino and uses a milk texture that's between that of a latte and a cappuccino, one that's slightly frothed but without the stiff foam.

To prepare a flat white, aerate your milk a bit longer than you typically would for a latte. When it's time to pour, don't groom your milk too aggressively. Allow some of the foam to settle on the top, then hold this back with a spoon and pour the smooth, creamy textured milk underneath into the espresso shots. The result will be a white coffee with the crema in a ring on top, still intact. Flat whites are typically made with strong espresso; for a truly authentic taste, you may even want to use a ristretto shot.

Tea lattes

Coffee isn't the only beverage that can be enhanced by the addition of steamed milk. Lattes based on brewed hot tea instead of coffee have gained much popularity in cafes in the past few decades. The most common of these is the chai latte, which typically uses a spiced Indian black tea as the base and is sweetened with honey. The London Fog is another popular drink, made with brewed Earl Grey tea and vanilla syrup. The Cape Town Fog is a caffeine-free variant of this beverage, using rooibos tea in place of the Earl Grey.

While there are some established recipes, you can make a latte using any tea base that you want. Brew it on the strong side—about half the water you'd usually use for the cup size, though you can adjust this up or down depending on your preferred ratio of milk to tea. Allow the tea to steep for 3-5 minutes then remove the bag and fill the remaining space with steamed milk. All the alternative milks discussed in the last chapter work well with tea lattes since you don't want a whole bunch of foam, anyway, just the creamy texture of the milk itself.

Because the flavor of green tea is so delicate, brewed green tea tends to be overpowered by the addition of milk, especially if you want to use non-dairy options. If you want a green tea latte, your best bet would be to buy Matcha powder, which gives you a concentrated dose of that grassy, sweet flavor green tea lovers seek. Each brand of powder will differ slightly in strength, so follow the ratio guidelines on the package and pour the powder into the cold milk just prior to steaming.

You can also mix tea with espresso. Chai lattes with an added espresso shot are known as dirty chais or chai chargers in café lingo. If you want to add espresso, it's best to use a strong black tea base, like a chai; the more delicate flavors of green tea tend to be overpowered completely by the addition of espresso.

Steam Wand Techniques

Getting the best possible milk from a steam wand is a multi-sensory experience. A skilled barista will listen to the sounds the milk is making to tell them when it has reached certain stages of steaming, feel the heat of the pitcher against their palm, and watch the surface to make sure that it has enough motion. Being able to interpret this information and use it to steam the milk perfectly for a given drink takes a lot of practice, but with time it becomes second-nature.

To steam properly, it can be helpful to understand how a steam wand works. When you turn on the wand, jets of steam shoot out of the rounded part at the end, called the tip. These jets essentially function the same way as a whisk, moving the milk in currents at the same time that it heats it. If you position the jets of steam right at the surface of the milk, they will also suck air into the milk as it's heated and rotated, which results in the tiny bubbles that form the foam.

The more air you allow into the milk, the more foam you will generate, and the more the milk will increase in volume. While a small amount of foam is almost always desirable, the ideal ratio of steamed milk to foam in your pitcher will depend on what kind of drink you're making. For a latte, the milk volume should increase by around 1/3; for a cappuccino, the milk volume should double.

When it's still on the steam wand, the milk and foam will be mixed together, but they will begin to separate as soon as they're removed from the wand. Keeping the milk in motion by swirling the pitcher can slow the separation, but in some techniques, it's preferred to allow the harder foam to separate out from the steamed milk, especially if you're making a cappuccino or flat white. As you develop your technique, you'll learn how much aeration produces the hardness and quantity of foam you like for various drinks and will be able to adjust accordingly.

The basic design of the steam wand is the same across espresso machines, though certain models will have different features and configurations. Any professional-level espresso machine will use a separate boiler for the steam wand than it does for brewing espresso, letting you pour shots and steam milk at the same time. These models also generally produce more pressure overall, giving you a faster steam. How you turn on the steam wand will also have an impact on your steaming technique. Some simply have an on/off switch, while others are turned on using an adjustable dial, which can be helpful in slowing the steam for more delicate drinks, like cortados and espresso macchiatos.

There are also aesthetic differences between steam wand designs. You want one that puts the wand at a comfortable angle for you to hold the pitcher while you're steaming. Most wands will be adjustable front-to-back, while others will also be able to rotate outwards to give you more space to work with between the pitcher and the group head. The angle of the wand in the pitcher is important to getting the right whirlpool motion during integration, so this can be an important consideration if you're shopping for an espresso machine and plan to use the steam wand frequently.

While getting the feel and nuance of steaming milk can take quite a bit of practice, the actual process of steaming a pitcher can be broken down into six easy steps. You will need to go through these steps rather quickly, however; especially on a professional steam wand, your milk will move through the steps in about the same amount of time it takes to brew a shot of espresso. Because of that, it's a good idea to know what you're looking for and basically how to achieve it before you turn on the wand for the first time.

Step 1: Prepare your pitcher

It's important to put the right amount of milk in your jug. Too much, and you may overflow the pitcher, and will end up wasting a lot of milk at the end of your drink; too little, and you won't be able to finish the drink properly. A good rule of thumb is to fill the jug about halfway. If you want a visual cue, the milk should be just at the lower point of the spout, where it forms into a "V."

If you're using a thermometer, you should clip it to the pitcher at this stage, as well. Make sure that the probe is pointed toward the center of the pitcher but off to one side, so it won't be touching the steam wand, which could give you inaccurate temperature readings. A thermometer is advisable at least while you're learning, until you get a feel for the different temperature ranges.

Step 2: Flush the line

Before you put your pitcher up to the steam wand, turn it on briefly, letting a hiss of steam out before turning it on again. This step accomplishes two things. First, it checks to make sure your steam wand is primed and ready to go. Second, it pushes out any milk from the previous pitcher that may have been sucked up into the line.

Step 3: Insert the wand

Put your pitcher up to the steam wand with the tip fully inserted before you turn it on. If you did it the other way, the steam would spray the surface of the milk, creating a large mess and making big bubbles in your milk. While you want to skim the surface of the milk with the tip to work air into it, you don't want to pull the wand out entirely at any point during the steaming, or you'll end up with a similar result. Hold the handle of the pitcher with one hand, and rest the other against the pitcher. It will get very hot as it steams, so you should make sure to hold the pitcher firmly in the handle hand in case it gets too hot for you to touch.

Step 4: Aeration

Up until it gets to around 100°F to 120°F, any air you work into the milk will be trapped as bubbles and will build your foam. Aeration is the process of allowing this air to work in and is also called "stretching" because it's the stage at which the milk grows in volume. When you first turn on the wand, you'll hear a hissing sound as the steam pushes through the milk. Slowly move the pitcher down until the tip is just at the surface. You'll know it's there because you'll hear a spitting sound, as well; that's the air being pulled into the wand.

If your milk begins to make a screeching sound, that's a sign you're not allowing enough air in. That noise is caused by the pressure of the steam trying to push its way to the surface of the milk. Once there are bubbles incorporated, the milk is less dense and the steam won't hiss on its way to the surface. It is worth noting that extremely thick materials may scream no matter how much they're aerated. Heavy cream, half and half, or seasonal ingredients like egg nog tend to steam a bit more loudly than other milks.

As you add more air and the milk expands, you'll need to lower your pitcher to keep the tip just at the surface. You should make all of these adjustments very subtle to avoid breaking the surface of the milk, which will allow too much air into the mix and ruin the microfoam you're building. The length of the aeration stage will depend on what kind of drink you're making. For a latte, it may only last a few seconds. For cortados and flat whites, you'll want to let it aerate a bit longer. For a cappuccino, you may want to aerate the milk all the way until it reaches 120°F.

Step 5: Integration

This stage is also known as "spinning" because of the ideal movement of the milk. The goal in this stage is to create a whirlpool motion in the pitcher, which combines the foam formed during aeration in with the steamed milk. Any particularly large bubbles formed during aeration are broken up during this stage, as well, which gives you the consistent texture of a well-steamed microfoam.

Submerge the tip of the steam wand fully into the milk, until it no longer makes a hissing or spitting noise. Tilt the pitcher slightly, keeping the steam wand roughly in the center of the milk. Experiment with different positions until you find the one that allows the milk to circulate of its own accord without you moving the pitcher. You ideally want to have a constant whirlpool motion until the milk is fully heated and ready to be removed from the wand.

The ideal temperature for most drinks is between 150°F and 165°F. If you're using a professional espresso machine, the milk heats up faster than your thermometer can keep up with; you'll probably want to remove the pitcher from the wand when it reads 140°F. It will rise into the correct range before the thermometer stops.

Step 6: Remove the pitcher

Turn off the steam wand before you remove the pitcher, or the sudden burst of air from the wand crossing the surface will ruin the hard work you've just done to craft your milk. As soon as you have removed the pitcher, wipe off the wand with a clean, damp towel to remove any milk residue, then briefly turn the steam wand on and off again to flush the line.

The finished product should have a smooth, glossy finish, with no visible bubbles. If there are a few bigger bubbles, you can tap them out by knocking the pitcher against the counter a few times. If you want to let your milk separate, you can leave it to sit for a few moments. If you don't, you should do what is known as "grooming." Swirl the milk inside the pitcher. Don't worry about being gentle; as long as the milk doesn't slosh over the side, you can use as much force as you would like. It will add more texture to the milk as well as keeping the foam and liquid from completely separating.

JESSICA SIMMS

Home Frothing

Learning the technique to steam milk correctly on a professional machine is tricky enough. Frothing at home, though, can provide its own unique set of challenges. While it's tricky to make good steamed milk using domestic appliances, it is still very possible if you're willing to put in the extra time to learn your equipment.

You can get a domestic espresso machine with a functional steam wand, some of which will even produce latte art-level microfoam. The steaming pressure will be the biggest difference between a commercial and a domestic espresso machine. Many home machines only have a single boiler, which provides pressure to both the group heads and the steam wand, meaning you can't use both at the same time and the overall steaming pressure will be lower. This means it will take longer for your milk to reach its optimal temperature, which can actually be an advantage for a relative beginner, giving you more time to stretch and incorporate the milk. It also means the thermometer will be able to keep up with changes in the milk's temperature, so you should wait to

32

remove it from the wand until the dial reads the temperature you want.

Many domestic espresso machines will have a froth assister on the steam wand. This compensates for the lower steam pressure generated by the smaller boiler. There is a small hole at the side of the froth assister that brings in the air. When using this style of steam wand, you'll want to position this hole at the surface during the aeration and submerge it for the incorporation, treating it like the nozzle on a traditional steam wand.

If you already have an espresso machine at home, the steam wand that comes with it will be your most reliable option for steaming milk, even if it has a relatively small boiler. While domestic steam wands do have a tendency to create more large bubbles than professional models, it is possible to get a decent microfoam with enough practice. If you don't already own an espresso machine, though, there are a variety of other less expensive options. Some of these will be better at generating foam than others, but some of them will give you milk that's as good or better than what comes off of domestic steam wands, and at a fraction of the cost of a full espresso machine.

Auto frothers

These machines will both heat and froth your milk, the same as a steam wand, but do so in a self-contained jug. The base of the jug contains a heating element and a whisk, often coming with different whisks that can be switched out depending on whether you're making a latte or a cappuccino, giving you some control over your level of froth.

A good auto frother will cost you anywhere from $50 to $150. The main difference you'll see between the price points is the quality of the foam, the speed of the heating, and the level of control you get. The Capresso frothXpress is a good choice if you're looking for thick, cappuccino-like foam. For the best latte milk, you might instead want to look at something from Breville. The higher-end models give you control over features like the temperature of the milk and can also make cold froth, something most auto frothers don't offer.

Frothing wands

If your budget has you looking in more of the $10 to $20 range, you may want to pick up a frothing wand. These hand-held and battery-powered appliances are essentially tiny, high-powered whisks. By spinning it just below the surface of the milk, you can incorporate air in a similar way to what's achieved on a steam wand, creating foam and texturing the milk.

Frothing wands do not create as close an approximation of microfoam as auto frothers. They tend to produce fairly large bubbles, and they won't make the proteins in the milk break down in the same way, so you won't get the noticeable increase in sweetness you find in milks steamed on a steam wand. It also will not heat the milk for you, meaning you'll have to do that first. You can microwave the milk in short bursts, but it will have a better flavor if you do it in a small saucepan on the stovetop. Keep the milk at low heat, until it's just bubbling, and make sure to keep it moving so it doesn't develop a skin on top. You can use the frothing wand throughout the process to incorporate air and build up the foam.

Despite their shortcomings, a frothing wand is the least expensive way to make yourself lattes and cappuccinos at home. If you're looking for a good brand, the wands put out by Kuissential give you some of the best foam you can get from a frothing wand. Bodum-brand frothers are also a good option.

Drink Preparation

The milk is only half the story when it comes to making your favorite café drink. You will also need to prepare the coffee, espresso, or tea that you'll be combining it with, along with any other flavorings you'll be adding. The order in which you prepare and add the ingredients to the drink can have a huge impact on the overall quality and flavor of the beverage.

If you're making an espresso-based drink, you ideally want to steam the milk and pour your shots at the same time. The crema on top of the espresso shot will begin to dissipate immediately, and you want to retain as much as possible. Since the milk will begin to separate with time, you also want to begin pouring it as soon as you can after steaming it. If it's not possible for you to make both at once, you should steam your milk first and prepare the espresso second. The milk can be groomed while you're waiting for your shots to pour, and you'll be able to start making your drink while the crema is still completely fresh.

If the espresso is the first thing added to a drink, brew it directly into the serving mug when you can. Some crema is inevitably lost when you transfer the shot from one container to another, so you want to avoid that step if you can. If you plan on adding any flavored syrups, put them in the cup, then brew the espresso into them. The heat of the coffee will melt the syrup and help the flavor to distribute evenly throughout the drink. If you're making a drink where the espresso is added last, you should brew into shot glasses, which will be easier to pour from than demitasse cups.

Free-pouring vs. spooning

Free-pouring refers to a drink preparation in which the milk is poured straight from the pitcher into the cup, letting the correct ratio of foam to milk be determined by the quality of the steaming. Spooning is just what it sounds like: using a spoon to add the foam after the milk has been poured, guaranteeing the correct ratio.

There are some drinks for which a certain technique is the industry standard across the board. Cortados and lattes are always free-poured, for example, while the foam in an espresso macchiato is always spooned on top, and the foam is always held back when pouring a flat white. For other drinks, though, there is some debate within the industry just which technique is best. You may see both methods being employed for latte macchiatos and cappuccinos, and both methods can yield delicious drinks.

When free-pouring, start with the spout of the steaming pitcher an inch or two above the surface of the espresso. The distance will cause the milk to sink below the coffee, leaving the crema undisturbed. Position the spout slightly off of center, but not so much that you're pouring down the side of the cup. Pour the milk in a slow, steady stream, gradually bringing the mouth of the pitcher closer to the surface of the drink. The closer the spout gets, the more of the white foam will sit on top of the espresso. This contrast of milk foam to crema is what can be used to create latte art; there is more on those techniques in the next chapter.

If you're spooning the foam into the cup, let your milk settle for a moment before you begin. When you're ready to pour, place a spoon at the spout of the pitcher to hold back the foam while you pour a thin, steady stream of steamed milk into your cup. When you've reached the desired level, use the spoon to scoop up the foam left in the pitcher and add it to the top of the drink. This technique will be a lot easier for beginners. It's less time-sensitive, for one thing, and also makes it easier to ensure you're getting the right ratio in your drink, even if your steaming technique isn't yet perfect.

Latte Art

It isn't completely clear when the practice of putting designs on the surface of a latte was started, or by whom. It began sometime in the mid-1980s in the United States, when David Schomer of Espresso Vivace started making art on his lattes, though an Italian man by the name of Luigi Lupi may have been the first to do it. Whoever started it, latte art quickly became a way to add more visual appeal to drinks.

Today, it is standard practice to put latte art on drinks in most cafes, both within the United States and around the world. There is more to latte art than just adding visual appeal to the drink. To get good latte art your individual components need to be at an optimal quality level. The espresso shots have to be poured correctly to generate persistent, dark crema suitable for making the designs. The steaming of the milk also has to be on point, with exactly the right amount of microfoam. Even if the design itself isn't perfect, the ability to get a strong contrast between the brown crema and the white milk is a sign that the drink was made correctly.

As is the case with steaming milk in general, getting the right pour in latte art is a matter of feel. Though the technique can be described to you, the best way to perfect it is through repeated practice, until the motions become second-nature and you are able to fine-tune your design by making subtle changes to your pour. Once you are able to master the initial motions required for the major designs, you will have the freedom to combine these techniques in any way you choose to create a truly personalized look.

Whatever design you decide to make, all latte art starts the same way: with a perfectly steamed pitcher of milk. There needs to be some microfoam on top of the milk, or else the steamed milk will just sink beneath the crema and you won't be able to get the contrast of colors used for the design. If the foam is too thick, however, it will sit on top of the crema in large blobs that make it difficult to get any definition.

If you're in the habit of steaming milk for multiple drinks at once, you won't want to do that when you start to make art; the distribution of steam and foam will be off in both drinks, preventing you from getting a clear design. All latte art must also be free-poured rather than spooned. It is typically the most common to see on lattes (hence the name) but you may also see it on cortados, or even free-poured cappuccinos. You can, in fact, make it on any drink where the espresso is added to the cup first and the milk is free-poured on top of it.

You'll see baristas who do latte art grooming their milk more aggressively than any other group. This is often necessary to maintain the right texture in the milk. The surface needs to be completely smooth—that glossy "white chrome" appearance discussed earlier in the book—and the separation of the foam and milk needs to be prevented as much as possible to allow the barista enough control to form the image. If the milk has been well-spun, much of the lighter foam will automatically be at the top of the jug and will pour out of the cup first, sinking below the crema so that the smooth, silky foam underneath can be used to create the art.

The kind of milk you choose will have a significant impact on the quality of the design, as well. When you're first learning, starting with 2% or whole cow's milk will make things easier, even if this isn't the milk you ultimately want to use in your drinks. The fat and protein content of these milks gives you a foam that's just right for latte art because it foams readily, but not too much. Skim milk will create a slightly thicker foam that will make it trickier to make fine lines and details.

It is certainly possible to make latte art using alternative milks; there are latte art competitions specifically for baristas using nondairy products, and these contests have showcased some incredible pieces of art made using soy, hemp, and even coconut milk. Just because it's possible doesn't mean it's easy, however. Getting latte art quality foam from alternative milk requires much more precision in both your steaming and your pouring. It's better to start learning with cow's milk then move on to alternative milks once you've perfected your technique. Keep in mind, too, that some milks simply won't give you good art, no matter how well you steam them. This is especially true of thinner products, like most cashew and almond milks, or low-fat versions of the milk types mentioned above.

The crema

Crema is the thin layer of pale brown foam that forms on the top of a well-poured shot of espresso. It forms through a similar process that creates the bubbles in steamed milk. Coffee beans naturally contain some trapped gasses, mostly carbon dioxide. As the heated water hits the ground coffee in the portafilter, the fats and other water-soluble components in ground beans are dissolved, releasing these gasses. The high pressure of the espresso brewing causes these released gasses to be temporarily suspended in the brewed beverage. Since it's less dense than the liquid portion of the espresso shot, it rises to the top of the drink in the cup.

For latte art, you will be concerned mostly with three qualities of the cream: its texture, its color, and its persistence. The texture should be even and smooth, with no visible bubbles, and no thin patches where the espresso is showing through. While good crema can have a range of colors, from a pale yellow to a deep golden brown, you want it to be on the darker side for latte art in order to get the maximum contrast between the crema and the milk. Finally, you want it to last long enough for you to complete your pour. All crema will eventually dissipate as the liquid espresso breaks down the foam and releases the trapped gasses. For latte art, you ideally want a crema that persists for 1-2 minutes if left undisturbed in the cup.

There is a phrase in the Italian coffee world outlining the four factors of crafting the perfect espresso, known colloquially as "the four M's" of espresso: la macinazione (the grind), la miscela (the blend), la macchina (the machine), and la mano (the hand). Getting great crema means paying attention to all four of these factors. With the grind, both the size and the timing are important. The ground coffee should have a consistent, fine texture, and should be ground immediately before brewing. The longer ground coffee sits, the more of its trapped gasses will escape on their own. Ground espresso that has sat for as little as 15 minutes before grinding will have lost about half of its volatile components, and you'll find little to no crema on the surface of your shots.

The blend, or the kinds of beans you use, is equally important. Not all coffees that make delicious espresso will produce the kind of crema you need for latte art. Light-roasted beans tend to have a thinner, lighter crema, so for latte art, you want something that's at a medium or dark roast. Many cafes will also put a bit of Robusta into their espresso blends; while its flavor is less complex than the more popular Arabica, a bit of Robusta adds color and thickness to the crema.

When it comes to your machine, the most important thing is that you're using high-quality equipment. Proper crema won't be produced if the machine isn't brewing at a high enough temperature. The Specialty Coffee Association of America states that a beverage isn't true espresso unless it's brewed using at least 9 bars of pressure. Make sure the machine is hot enough before brewing, as well; the water should ideally be between 195°F and 205°F. Quality equipment means using a good grinder, too. While other brewing methods can be prepared just as well using a blade grinder, for espresso you need a burr grinder that's capable of small and precise adjustments.

Finally, there's the technique of the barista, expressed in the adage as "the hand." An experienced barista will know how to tamp the grinds correctly to get an even pour. For latte art, you'll often want a brew time that's slightly on the longer side, closer to 30 seconds than 20. Knowing how to adjust the grind and the tamping pressure to make these kinds of adjustments is a learned skill and, like crafting good microfoam, takes practice to master.

However well the shot is poured, crema won't last forever. You want to use your time efficiently once you've started brewing your espresso. Brewing your espresso shot directly into your serving mug is highly recommended; not only does this save time but it limits the disturbance to the crema, helping it to last longer. Ideally, you will be able to brew the shots while you're steaming the milk so that both finish at the same time. Even with effective grooming, steamed milk can only sit so long before the foam starts to separate and fall, so you don't want to leave it sitting for too long, but if you have to finish one before the other finish the milk first so you can use the espresso shot immediately.

The basic pour

The technique of the initial pour will be the same no matter which design you're making, but you'll want to position the spout differently for some designs, so it's a good idea to plan your pattern before you begin the process. Tilt your cup slightly before you start pouring. This both expands the surface area of the shot and makes it easier for you to see the surface as you work. For most patterns, you'll want to begin your pour slightly off of center in the direction of the tilt, moving the pour gradually to the middle as you straighten the cup.

The speed of your pour is important for a number of reasons. First of all, it is a matter of timing. If you pour the milk too quickly you'll fill the cup before you have time to finish your design; if you pour the milk too slowly, the stream is likely to break, causing blobs and gaps in the art. A slow and steady stream also loosens up the crema, allowing it to move more freely and letting you create better designs. Start pouring from a few inches above the surface of the milk, with a stream narrow enough that it sinks straight through the crema without breaking it.

As you're filling and straightening the cup, gradually lower the pitcher, as well. When the drink is about half full, you should have the cup returned to level, and the spout of the pitcher almost touching the surface of the drink. At this point, you should start to see the white foam begin resting on the surface. You'll know it's time to start pouring the pattern because the crema around your pour will begin to lighten. Seeing white tracers of foam where you pour is also a good indication you're ready to pour your design.

Controlling the flow of the milk is often the most difficult thing for beginners to master when it comes to their latte art technique. Changing the speed of your pour will affect the thickness of your lines. A faster pour will make thicker lines, while a slower pour will make them thinner. While you can intentionally alter the speed of your pour to achieve a certain effect, doing so unintentionally will result in inconsistencies in your design. Making smooth motions with the pitcher will give you the best definition on your lines.

The possibilities for latte art are only limited by your technique and your imagination. A quick Google image search will show you all the incredible things people can do with more advanced latte art techniques. When you're first starting out, though, there are a few basic patterns that you'll want to learn. Mastering the techniques employed in the designs that follow will give you the skills you need when you're ready to take your art to the next level.

Monk's head

The simplest design is known as the monk's head. This is the first pattern you should learn when you're beginning to do latte art. Because doesn't require any motion of the pitcher, it's a good shape for practicing your symmetry, positioning, and contrast. The end shape will be a circle of white foam, ideally in the center of the cup, with a notch at the top where the pitcher mouth was positioned.

Start your pour as described above. When the cup is about 2/3 full, bring the spout of the pitcher down until it's nearly touching the surface of the drink. You should start to see a growing white circle inside the brown ring of crema. You don't need to move the spout; as more milk is poured into the cup, it will naturally push the foam that's already there outward, increasing the size of the monk's head until the drink is full and you remove the pitcher.

Heart

Once you've mastered the basic monk's head, you can move up to the heart. This pattern follows the same basic principle, but instead of keeping your pitcher steady you'll wiggle it slightly from side to side as you're pouring, creating lines of white foam separated by dark crema. Like with the monk's head, you want to position the design basically in the center of the cup. Keep the pitcher steady during the initial pouring phase. When the cup is about ½ full, lower the pitcher to the surface.

It's at this point you'll begin to wiggle the pitcher gently from side to side. You've no doubt seen baristas doing this in your local coffee shop. The center point of the arc should not move once you've started pouring. Like with the monk's head, the milk you're pouring in will push the milk ahead of it out into a striated circle, so you don't need to move the pitcher to get the design to spread over the surface. The more you wiggle the pitcher from side to side, the wider the design will be. When you're ready to finish the design, pull the pitcher across the circle in a straight line, still pouring, then lift your pitcher when you've reached the bottom of the foam. The notch where you were pouring will be the top of the heart, and the place where you lifted the pitcher will be the point.

Rosetta

This leaf-shaped pattern is perhaps the best-known late art design. It builds off of the wiggle technique you use in the heart, so you want to perfect your hearts before moving on to a rosetta. Start the same way, pouring a slow steady stream from a few inches above the surface, but when you bring the spout down to start the design, you want to position the spout toward one side of the cup. Start making the same wiggling motion you would for a heart, but instead of holding the pitcher in place, move slowly across the cup. The foam will leave a series of white lines behind, separated by dark crema. To finish the design, drawn the pitcher back through the lines to your starting point, more quickly this time, pouring as you go to form the stem between the leaves.

Just like with the heart, the size of your wiggle will determine how wide the leaves are in the cup. Because the bottom leaves are at the bottom of the cup, the force of the milk that follows them will push them out and around the sides, naturally making the bottom of the rosetta wider than the top; if you want a more dramatic narrowing, you can also reduce the size of your wiggle as you go. How quickly you move the pitcher from the bottom of the cup to the top will determine the spacing of the leaves. The faster you do it, the more space you'll have, and the lower the density of the leaves will be. Ideally, you want your pacing to be the same throughout the pour so the space between the top leaves and the bottom leaves is consistent.

The biggest mistake most beginners make with the rosetta is not moving the pitcher enough from one side of the cup to the other. This results in designs that look more like a slightly elongated heart, with the leaves smushed together so that they look more like sticks. Many people will also finish the design off with a heart at the top, which can be a great technique for finishing the drink if you've moved from one side to the other too quickly; continue to wiggle the pitcher with the spout in one place until the drink is full enough to finish the design.

Tulip

Here is where the patterns start to get a bit more complicated. A well-crafted tulip is a beautiful and intricate pattern with a lot of potential for creative variation, but it requires a skilled hand to produce effectively, with a steady pour and a perfect pitcher of milk. Unlike the designs above that can be made in a single pour, the tulip will require you to raise and lower your pitcher multiple times. If your foam is too thick, this can result in misshapen blobs; if it's too thin, too much milk will submerge and the pattern won't come out. Even experienced baristas usually need a lot of practice until they can consistently coordinate the series of pours required.

Start out as you normally would, pouring the milk from a few inches above the surface until the cup is around half full. Bring the spout to the surface at around the center of the cup and make a small dot of foam, without any wiggling, like you would do in a monk's head. Now stop the pour, move the pitcher back slightly, and pour another small dot of foam. Nudge it forward slightly, encouraging it to flatten and move toward the first dot. As the new dot pours, the first will be pushed toward the bottom of the cup, flattening into the "leaves" of the tulip. Stop pouring, shift back, and repeat. Most people stop after the third circle, but you can add as many as will fit into your cup.

When you're pouring the last of the dots, instead of simply lifting the pitcher when it's finished forming, bring it down through the entire design, like you would do with a rosetta or heart. This separates the leaves and connects the design together. Changing the speed of your pour will alter the size and spread of the individual leaves of the tulip. The dot at the top will be the flower. You can add pedals to it if you'd like by wiggling the pitcher during the last pour only.

Swan

Learning to make all of the designs above will get you familiar with the different wrist and pitcher motions you can use to alter the appearance of your latte art pattern. Once you've perfected those techniques, you can bring them together into a more elaborate design. The most common of these is the swan, which uses techniques from the rosetta, the tulip, and the heart all in one pattern.

Like the rosetta or heart, the swan can be created in a single pour. Fill the cup from a distance about halfway, then bring the pitcher down to the surface and make a rosetta on one side of the cup. When you finish it, instead of bringing the pitcher down the center from top to bottom like you normally would, bring the line down the side closest to the edge of the cup. This forms the wing of the swan.

Once you're at the base of the wing, hold the pitcher in place and wiggle it side to side, as you would to make a heart. This creates the body of the swan. Use a tight pattern to do this, and nudge it forward slightly like you would with the dots in a tulip. If you make the body too big, it can distort the wing and leave you too little room to make the neck and head. Once it's done, stop wiggling the pitcher and continue pouring while you drag it toward you, forming the neck. When you reach the top of the cup, bend it down in a "U" shape. Keep the pitcher relatively close to the crema the entire time you do this. If the foam sinks under the crema, the line of the neck will be broken. This step might sound simple, but will be a test of your steady hand and your steaming skills. You'll need a perfect, smooth microfoam to get a trailing line of foam that doesn't glob but is firm enough to rest on the crema.

Finally, it's time to make the head. Again make the motions of a heart, though on a smaller scale this time than when you made the body. When it's big enough, pull the pitcher down through so that the point of the heart makes the tip of the beak. As you can see, this pattern has a lot more steps than any of the above. You'll need to consider how to best use the space on the surface of your drink before you start pouring the milk. It also tests your portioning skills. Use too much foam for the wing, and you won't have enough to finish the head nicely—or you'll run out of room in the cup and end up overflowing your mug. The pattern is impressive once you master the techniques, however, and is a good way to get started with more advanced patterns.

Etching

Some of the things you can do with free-poured latte art are truly amazing, but you'll be dealing primarily with outlines and shapes; fine details are exceptionally difficult to work in using free-pouring techniques. If you see lattes that are decorated with drawings of cartoon characters or a portrait of George Washington, this has been accomplished with a technique known as etching.

You can think of etching as drawing on the surface of the drink. Typically, the barista will start by free-pouring the general outline or shape of the figure in foam. Once that's done, they'll brew a fresh shot of espresso and dip the tip of the milk thermometer in the crema, then use this to paint the details onto the foam outline. Some people will also use chocolate or caramel syrup to add different shades or effects to the design. For especially fine details, they may use a toothpick instead of a thermometer.

Since the free-pouring design of an etched pattern is often very simple, it will serve you better to use a bit of a stiffer foam when you're practicing this technique. You'll need time to etch your design on the surface, and you want the microfoam to stick around long enough the design still looks nice when it's finished. You do inevitably sacrifice a bit of quality for appearance since espresso drinks are best enjoyed immediately after they're prepared, but it can be a fun technique to play around with as you're expanding your latte art knowledge.

Investing in Your Coffee

Most people think of espresso drinks as belonging to the domain of the professional barista. The cost of those drinks prepared in a coffee shop can be a bit much for daily consumption, however, especially if you order your drinks made with a non-dairy milk. As you're deciding whether home frothing equipment would be worth the investment, consider its cost in lattes. An espresso machine may still be out of reach, but the $20 you'd spend on a frothing wand might get you six drinks—meaning it will start paying for itself in less than a week, if you're a daily drinker—and even a $150 auto frother is at most equivalent to a two-month supply, for a daily latte or cappuccino drinker.

Automatic coffee makers with built-in steamers that claim to make drinks like cappuccinos and lattes never quite achieve that silky texture and depth of flavor that you'll get from a drink that's been prepared properly. As is the case with coffee brewers, you'll get better-tasting drinks out of a $30 Aeropress and a $20 frothing wand than you will from a $250 machine that claims to do it all but does none of it especially well.

The level of equipment you'll need to invest in will depend on how far you plan to develop your craft. If your goal is to make espresso drinks that taste comparable to the ones you'd order in a café, an auto frother will serve your purposes just fine. This is especially true for drinkers of almond or cashew milk since their thin texture means they won't get much foam from an espresso machine steam wand, either. If you want to experiment with latte art, however, you'll need to purchase an espresso machine. You can use a single-boiler machine so long as it can generate enough steam pressure to create crema on your shots and microfoam in your milk.

As is the case with many skills, practice is the key to perfecting your milk steaming technique. Don't get frustrated if it turns out poorly on your first attempt. Use all of your senses to assess what went well and what mistakes you made during the process. Think about whether the milk made the right sounds as you were steaming it; if it made a loud, high-pitched noise, you likely didn't allow enough air in during the aeration phase. Examine the surface of the milk, looking for large bubbles, which could point to too much air being worked in, or air being worked in too late in the process. Consider how it tastes in the cup, as well. If there's a bitter, flat aftertaste, the milk was likely over-steamed and ended up scorching; if it's grainy or dull, it likely wasn't steamed enough.

Just like brewing your own coffee, learning to steam your own milk consistently is a skill with tangible rewards. Your morning cappuccino will taste all the sweeter when you're able to enjoy it in the comfort of your own kitchen and have the freedom to experiment with different tastes and textures can expand your coffee horizons, helping you to find your perfect cup.

Win a free

kindle
OASIS

Let us know what you thought of this book to enter the sweepstake at:

http://booksfor.review/steamingmilk

Want to

supercharge

your coffee knowledge?

Turn this page...

Also available by
Jessica Simms

Blending Coffee

Your Guide to Coffee Blends and the Perfect Cup

JESSICA SIMMS

I know **coffee**

Harvesting,
Blending,
Roasting,
Brewing,
Grinding,
& Tasting
Coffee

JESSICA SIMMS

Harvesting Coffee

Life of a Coffee Bean from Planting to Processing

JESSICA SIMMS

Roasting Coffee

How to Roast Green Coffee Beans like a Pro!

JESSICA SIMMS

Brewing & Grinding Coffee

How to Make Good Coffee at Home

JESSICA SIMMS

The
I know coffee
series

Tasting Coffee

Coffee Cupping Techniques to Unleash the Bean!

JESSICA SIMMS

Making Crema

The Art and Science of the Perfect Espresso Shot

JESSICA SIMMS

Printed in Great Britain
by Amazon